W9-BSC-851

John Brown

Abolitionist

Colonial Leaders

Lord Baltimore
English Politician and Colonist

Benjamin Banneker
American Mathematician and Astronomer

Sir William Berkeley
Governor of Virginia

William Bradford
Governor of Plymouth Colony

Jonathan Edwards
Colonial Religious Leader

Benjamin Franklin
American Statesman, Scientist, and Writer

Anne Hutchinson
Religious Leader

Cotton Mather
Author, Clergyman, and Scholar

Increase Mather
Clergyman and Scholar

James Oglethorpe
Humanitarian and Soldier

William Penn
Founder of Democracy

Sir Walter Raleigh
English Explorer and Author

Caesar Rodney
American Patriot

John Smith
English Explorer and Colonist

Miles Standish
Plymouth Colony Leader

Peter Stuyvesant
Dutch Military Leader

George Whitefield
Clergyman and Scholar

Roger Williams
Founder of Rhode Island

John Winthrop
Politician and Statesman

John Peter Zenger
Free Press Advocate

Revolutionary War Leaders

John Adams
Second U.S. President

Samuel Adams
Patriot

Ethan Allen
Revolutionary Hero

Benedict Arnold
Traitor to the Cause

John Burgoyne
British General

George Rogers Clark
American General

Lord Cornwallis
British General

Thomas Gage
British General

King George III
English Monarch

Nathanael Greene
Military Leader

Nathan Hale
Revolutionary Hero

Alexander Hamilton
First U.S. Secretary of the Treasury

John Hancock
President of the Continental Congress

Patrick Henry
American Statesman and Speaker

William Howe
British General

John Jay
First Chief Justice of the Supreme Court

Thomas Jefferson
Author of the Declaration of Independence

John Paul Jones
Father of the U.S. Navy

Thaddeus Kosciuszko
Polish General and Patriot

Lafayette
French Freedom Fighter

James Madison
Father of the Constitution

Francis Marion
The Swamp Fox

James Monroe
American Statesman

Thomas Paine
Political Writer

Molly Pitcher
Heroine

Paul Revere
American Patriot

Betsy Ross
American Patriot

Baron Von Steuben
American General

George Washington
First U.S. President

Anthony Wayne
American General

Famous Figures of the Civil War Era

John Brown
Abolitionist

Jefferson Davis
Confederate President

Frederick Douglass
Abolitionist and Author

Stephen A. Douglas
Champion of the Union

David Farragut
Union Admiral

Ulysses S. Grant
Military Leader and President

Stonewall Jackson
Confederate General

Joseph E. Johnston
Confederate General

Robert E. Lee
Confederate General

Abraham Lincoln
Civil War President

George Gordon Meade
Union General

George McClellan
Union General

William Henry Seward
Senator and Statesman

Philip Sheridan
Union General

William Sherman
Union General

Edwin Stanton
Secretary of War

Harriet Beecher Stowe
Author of Uncle Tom's Cabin

James Ewell Brown Stuart
Confederate General

Sojourner Truth
Abolitionist, Suffragist, and Preacher

Harriet Tubman
Leader of the Underground Railroad

Famous Figures of the Civil War Era

John Brown

Abolitionist

Virginia Brackett

Arthur M. Schlesinger, jr.
Senior Consulting Editor

Chelsea House Publishers

Philadelphia

CHELSEA HOUSE PUBLISHERS
Editor-in-Chief Sally Cheney
Director of Production Kim Shinners
Production Manager Pamela Loos
Art Director Sara Davis
Production Editor Diann Grasse

Staff for *JOHN BROWN*
Editor Sally Cheney
Associate Art Director Takeshi Takahashi
Series Design Keith Trego
Layout by D&G Limited, LLC

The Chelsea House World Wide Web address is
http://www.chelseahouse.com

First Printing
1 3 5 7 9 8 6 4 2

Library of Congress Cataloging-in-Publication Data

Brackett, Virginia.
    John Brown / Virginia Brackett.
       p. cm. — (Famous figures of the Civil War era)
    Includes bibliographical references and index.
    ISBN 0-7910-6408-5 (alk. paper) — ISBN 0-7910-6409-3 (pbk. :
    alk. paper)
       1. Brown, John, 1800-1859—Juvenile literature. 2. Abolitionists—
    United States—Biography—Juvenile literature. 3. Antislavery
    movements—United States—History—19th century—Juvenile
    literature. [1. Brown, John, 1800-1859. 2. Abolitionists.] I. Title.
    II. Series.

E451 .B79 2001
973.7'116'092—dc21
[B]   2001028762

Contents

Men, women, and children were taken from Africa and brought to the United States. They were then sold to plantation owners in the South. Slaves worked for little or no money in the fields and homes of their owners, and they had no rights or freedoms. This arrangement benefited the plantation owners and was an important part of the Southern economy. Plantation owners could operate their farms with very few expenses.

A Young Man with a Mission

In the year 1800, Owen and Ruth Brown awaited the birth of their baby. The United States was still a new country. Only 24 years had passed since the signing of the Declaration of Independence. It declared the United States free from England, the country from which settlers had crossed the Atlantic Ocean to come to America. In the Revolutionary War, Americans defeated the British, who claimed America as their land. Owen Brown's father had died in the Revolution. After the war, Owen's ancestors lived for years in Connecticut. If his new baby was a boy, Owen planned to name him John, after Owen's great-grandfather.

On May 9, 1800, John Brown was born in Torrington, Connecticut. Owen and Ruth had two sons before John, but they both died. Also before John was born, the Browns had adopted a son named Levi Blakesley. They also had a daughter, Ruth. With John, the Browns had three healthy children.

The year 1800 held another important event, this one involving slaves. Of the five million people in the United States and the territories, not all were free. More than half a million were slaves. Most slaves were from Africa, and they were forced to work for Southern white people. They bought and owned the slaves. Slaves often were beaten. Husbands, wives, and children could be sold to different owners. In the year of John's birth, 1,000 slaves in the state of Virginia staged an uprising called Gabriel's Slave **Rebellion**. The slaves were soon captured, and their leader, Gabriel, was hanged along with 14 of his followers. The rebellion caused many whites to consider ending slavery. Most who wanted to end slavery lived in the Northern states and territories.

The Browns remained in Connecticut for five years. John's two brothers, Salmon and Oliver were born there. In 1805 they moved to the state of Ohio. John remembered the trip for a long time. Camping out in the dark was exciting for a young boy. Ohio was still a frontier where Native Americans lived. John liked the Native Americans, although many people feared them. They taught John their language, and they taught his father to skin deer. As an adult, John wrote that a Native American boy once gave him

When the American colonies first formed, some British people were willing to work as servants. By the 1600s, servants were difficult to find. Families needing workers turned to the use of African slaves instead. Over 200 years, slavers kidnapped 10 to 11 million Africans from their homes. They were loaded into crowded ships and taken to different countries. About 600,000 Africans arrived in chains to what is now the United States. A slave sold for about $2,000.

A Native American is shown wearing traditional clothes
and jewelry.

a yellow marble. When he later lost the marble, he became very upset. It was one of the few toys John had that belonged only to him.

The Browns settled in an area of Ohio called Hudson. Hudson sat in the middle of 6,000 square miles known as the "Western Reserve." Those acres lay along Lake Erie, just west of Pennsylvania. The Reserve became a center for wool production and for actions against slavery, called antislavery movements. Antislavery acts occurred often during the 41 years that John lived in or close to Hudson.

Owen Brown became a successful tanner, or person who processed animal skins or hides for use in clothing and other articles. Owen also owned a farm and raised cattle and sheep. As John grew older, he learned all about his father's businesses. He also learned to hate slavery as much as Owen did.

The family had a sturdy, safe home and plenty of food. Still, John did not enjoy a happy childhood. After the birth of Frederick in 1807, his mother lost her good health. After Ruth gave birth to a girl in 1808, both she and the baby soon died. John lost his beloved mother when he was only eight years old. That left Owen to run the tannery while also caring for John, his five other sisters and brothers, and Levi. It proved an impossible task. He married a new wife, Sally Root. John never became close to Sally, but he always helped the family.

John did not have time for much school because he had to work in the tannery. He did learn to read and later borrowed books from others. At age 10, John took a special interest in history. He enjoyed playing with the other children and with his pet squirrel. One day the squirrel bit John, then ran away into the woods. Another pet, a lamb, became sick and died. John would write later about these losses. He said his childhood helped him understand things. One of those things was that whatever God gave to him, God could also take from him. Like his father Owen, John became very religious.

Before long, arguments among different groups over who would control parts of the United States grew into a war. By 1811 the Native Americans feared the loss of their lands. The British also wanted some land. They joined some Native American tribes, mostly a group called the Shawnees, to fight the United States. The War of 1812 began. Owen Brown did not choose sides. To him, war simply meant more business. Soldiers needed his leather products to wear and his animals for food. As for John, he viewed war as a waste of energy and life. When he grew older, John could be forced to drill with the troops. Instead he chose to pay a fine, which allowed him to avoid that duty. For years, he refused even to buy a gun.

John made another important decision as a teenager. He vowed to fight slavery. At age 15, he delivered some cattle to soldiers in a distant town. There he enjoyed kind treatment by a man who asked John to join his guests at dinner. He praised John's clever remarks during the

Shown here are U.S. Army officers on during the War of 1812. The war ended with the Treaty of Ghent, which restored relations between the United States and Great Britain.

evening. But John's attention was on another boy, a slave who served his master and the guests. John's host beat the boy in front of everyone. He struck him with a small fireplace shovel. John later wrote about his anger at this treatment, saying it caused him to "swear eternal war with slavery." He would remain true to that promise.

Upon returning home to Ohio, John felt that God called him to attend a school for preachers. John talked with his father about his feelings. He explained that he needed to leave. This would affect Owen's business, where John was a foreman in charge of other men. Still, Owen did not argue to keep his son at home.

A tall, polite young man, John traveled to Plainfield, Massachusetts. He had heard of a school run by a man named Reverend Moses Hallock. The reverend had schooled several well-known preachers. He welcomed John who seemed perfect preacher material. John had never gambled or danced. He proved to be one of the most serious students. John took great pride in keeping himself clean and neat. He always brushed his hair straight back from his forehead. He brought along a smooth piece of leather that he had tanned to repair any holes in his boots.

In spite of his plans, John would not be a minister. His eyes became irritated and red from infection, and he had to return to Ohio. He worked as his father's foreman and moved into a cabin with his adopted brother, Levi. When not working or cooking at home, John studied arithmetic. He had decided to work someday as a surveyor, a person who measures out land into plots.

One night Levi and John answered a knock at the door. There stood a runaway slave. As many that lived in the North might do, the young men offered the slave shelter. Then Levi went into town for supplies. Before long, John and the slave heard horses. John helped his guest climb through a window and told him to hide in the brush. Luckily, the horses belonged to some neighbors who just rode by. John began to search for the boy. He later wrote, "I heard his heart thumping before

John Brown once witnessed the beating of a slave and from that point on pledged "eternal war with slavery."

I reached him." According to John, the slave moved on in his search for freedom.

When John later wrote about his experiences, he enjoyed making them dramatic. Some accused him of exaggerating to make a good story. However, John told the truth when he declared that the event with the runaway slave made him swear again to battle slavery. Like Owen, John was an **abolitionist**. Abolitionists believed slavery must be abolished, or done away with. The Browns also believed that all people in America should enjoy equal rights.

As John matured, he became a careful manager. This made him popular with men much older than himself. Although he spent all of his time in the tannery, he hoped one day to raise sheep, cattle, and horses. The one thing that he lacked was a wife. His father had served as his model in many ways, and John admired him as a family man. Over the years, Owen Brown had three wives and at least 16 children. John also wanted a large family, but in his late teen years, he wondered whether he would find the perfect match. As it turned out, he would not have to wait much longer.

This advertisement for the abolition of slavery was made for the Antislavery Society, which was formed in 1831. The poster shows African Americans going from freedom in their country to slavery in the United States. It also depicts the conflict between slavery and the right to liberty.

Thriving
Business

Owen Brown's business continued to grow. John and Levi worked so much that they needed help at home with the baking and cleaning. A widowed neighbor named Mrs. Amos Lusk came to work for the boys. She began to bring her daughter, Dianthe, along. Dianthe was one year younger than John. A quiet girl, she sang hymns and rarely laughed. When she did speak, she was blunt, saying exactly what was on her mind. John liked Dianthe's direct speech and strong religious beliefs. When John asked Dianthe to marry him, she agreed. On June 21, 1820, the couple began a marriage that lasted 12 years and produced seven children.

Life changed little for Mr. and Mrs. John Brown. John continued to work for Owen, while Dianthe cared for the house. On July 25, 1821, John Brown Jr. was born. John enjoyed his work routine and his new duties as husband and father.

Within a year, a second son, Jason, came along. John decided the family needed more room than the log cabin allowed. Business was good, and John had money. He wanted to move into his own home, so in 1824, he built a new wood house for his growing family. He also designed a garden and planted a fruit tree orchard. Within a few months, a third son joined the Browns. John and Dianthe named him Owen, after John's father. People for miles around knew of the successful tanner and family man. By 1829 two more babies, Frederick and Ruth, had arrived.

John had a reputation for strictness. His family dressed in somber brown clothing, and they ate well, but sparingly. A devoutly religious person,

John believed in whipping his children with a switch made from a tree stem when they misbehaved. However, he also held them at night and sang their favorite songs. His children later described John as a loving father. Although he punished wrongdoings, John did not enjoy it. On one occasion after switching John Jr. he allowed the boy to use the switch on his own bare back. He never threatened his children, but he did demand their obedience.

The workers in John's tannery had to attend church each Sunday. They also had to join the Browns each morning for a Bible reading. John demanded loyalty and honesty from his workers. Once, he caught a worker stealing a calf hide. He told the worker that if he would be honest in the future, John would not call the law. However, he also issued a command that no one at work speak to the thief. According to some, the thief remained with John for two additional months. Then he went out on his own to become a good citizen.

Like his father, John did not mind moving. In the spring of 1825 he decided to take his family to the neighboring state of Pennsylvania. They settled in a town called Randolph, where John set up a tannery. The country was still wild with many deer and bear. John purchased 25 acres of land and built a huge double cabin. He often invited his tannery workers to share a meal with his family. Sometimes up to 15 people would gather around the Browns's table.

During the cold winter months, Native Americans often set up a camp just outside Randolph. When they came to John for hay and water for their horses, he did not turn them away. This angered some of his neighbors. They asked John and his workers to help them drive the Native Americans away. John refused. He also took in escaped slaves. As the children grew, he talked with them about the evils of slavery.

John's good reputation was honored in 1828. He became Randolph's postmaster, the first in the region. This meant that John would be trusted to handle everyone's mail. He also brought the first purebred cattle to that part of Pennsylvania and kept a big flock of sheep. He established Sunday morning worship services for everyone and started a school. In the winter, classes met at the Brown house, and in the summer, at another citizen's house.

In 1828 the antislavery movement strengthened. A young man named William Lloyd Garrison spoke against slavery at a meeting in Boston. He was leaving New England to become editor of an antislavery newspaper in Baltimore, Maryland. Over the years, John read Garrison's paper, the *Liberator*. It taught John much about the antislavery movement.

Also in 1828, Dianthe began to show signs of mental illness, a problem that worsened over time. John remained devoted to his wife. During her bouts of illness, he stayed awake at night and made sure that the fire did not die out and cause her a chill. She had another baby boy in 1830 who remained unnamed for a time. Both John

William Lloyd Garrison was an abolitionist and publisher of the *Liberator,* a
newspaper that supported the immedi-
ate end to slavery. He was also a founder
of the American Antislavery Society.

and Dianthe continued their devotion to anti-slavery ideals.

Not everyone in Massachusetts believed in abolition. Several abolitionists came under attack. Hot tar was spread over their bodies and feathers shaken onto the sticky mess. After being "tarred and feathered," the abolitionists were driven from their homes. Meanwhile, slavery continued to catch the attention of the nation. In 1831 a Virginia slave named Nat Turner led a revolt. The U.S. military finally captured Turner and his followers. That incident claimed the lives of 57 white people. The numbers of blacks killed and executed were not carefully kept, but between 40 and 100 died. Nat Turner hanged for his part as leader.

The Browns also experienced death in 1831. Their four-year old son, Frederick, died. The parents buried their son, then gave Frederick's name to their unnamed baby that had been born the previous year. One more year passed, and in 1832, a newborn boy died. Dianthe became very ill, and in August she died. Like John's mother, Dianthe Brown gave birth to seven children, lost two, and died after 12 years of marriage.

John had five children to care for on his own–John Jr., Jason, Owen, Ruth, and baby Frederick. He had to hire a housekeeper. That woman brought her sister, Mary, along with her to spin thread and make clothes for the Brown family. At 16 years of age, Mary Ann Day was a large girl not afraid of hard work. On July 11, 1833, John and Mary wed, even though she was half his age. Mary would live with John until his death and have a total of 13 sons and daughters. As with Dianthe, not all the children would survive. The six who survived to adulthood were Sarah, Anne, Ellen, Watson, Salmon, and Oliver. Of those six, only four would live longer than their mother.

During 1834, John wrote a letter to his brother, Frederick, making clear his abolitionist beliefs. He wrote that he wanted to help his "poor fellowmen" who were in "bondage." One

A fugitive slave family is shown crossing the Rappahannock River. Slaves could stop for help at safe houses in the Underground Railroad along the route to the North.

part of his plan was to adopt an ex-slave child. He and Mary wanted to raise that child as their own and give him a good education. The second part of his plan was to "get a school a-going here

John's home could be thought of as a stop on the **Underground Railroad**. That name was given to a system of safe houses where runaway slaves could stop for help. Although not a real railroad, it was described by words usually used when speaking of trains. The slaves were "passengers," the homes where they stayed were "stations," and their guides were "conductors." In reality, not very many slaves escaped by way of the Underground Railroad. However, the Underground Railroad became an important symbol of antislavery, and some of its conductors became famous.

for the blacks." He asked Frederick whether he and others in his old hometown of Hudson would help him set up such a school. He felt that the school could act "on slavery like firing powder confined in rock."

Such a plan could be dangerous. In nearby Connecticut, John's birthplace, slavery was already against the law. Even so, some citizens did not want blacks to be educated. A state law said that schools in one town could not educate blacks from another town without a vote by the town leaders. One woman named Prudence Crandall went to jail under this law. Some of her neighbors then set fire to her house. Although John never built his school, he continued to think of ways to help the abolitionist movement.

General Winfield Scott and his men entered Mexico City in 1847 and defeated Mexican troops in the last battle of the Mexican-American War. At the end of the war, the Treaty of Guadalupe Hidalgo set the southern boundary of Texas and gave New Mexico and California to the United States.

A Time of Loss and Gain

In 1835 the Browns moved to Franklin, Ohio. Mary's first baby, Sarah, was a year old, and Watson would be born later in 1835. John hoped to take advantage of increasing trade between the East and the Midwest to help support his family. Like others, John believed that a land "boom" would soon occur in Ohio. Many thought that thousands of people would move to the Western Reserve. Believing in the importance of progress, John even helped with the digging of the Mahoning Canal. It had been designed to link the Western Reserve to Pennsylvania. Along with 21 other men, John created the

Franklin Land Company. He borrowed money to buy farms and other land around Franklin Mills, a town not far from Hudson. John planned to make a huge profit selling his land to settlers. He also built a new tannery.

In 1836, however, John's dream collapsed. The government announced that people could no longer pay for land with paper money that came from banks. They had to pay instead with gold or silver that few people had. This caused the Panic of 1837. The country was in a **depression** and many people could not find work. The unstable conditions halted the Mahoning Canal construction. John was one of many whose lands were now worthless, and he faced bankruptcy. If he declared himself bankrupt, he would have to publicly announce that he had lost his money and could not pay his debts.

At the same time, John had problems with his local church. Most Northern churches allowed blacks to attend services, where they sat in the back of the room. John could not accept this.

One Sunday he asked some blacks to join him in his family pew. Many churchgoers became angry. Not everyone in Ohio wanted equality for African Americans like John did. Before long, the Browns stopped attending services. They remained deeply religious, worshipping in their home. John felt that God was testing him, and he was determined to pass the test. He decided to leave Franklin and return to Hudson.

By 1837 the Browns had two more sons, Charles and Salmon, to feed. John had begun herding cattle 600 miles to the East Coast to earn money. This caused him to be away from home for long periods. During his first trip to Connecticut, he sold a herd of cattle and bought 10 sheep. He tried to borrow money from a New York bank to pay his many debts but was not successful. John continued to work as a herder in Ohio for several years, but he remained in debt. He tried to cheer Mary, telling her in one 1839 letter, "Tomorrow may be a much brighter day."

Eventually, some people began to regain their property. Workmen at last completed the Mahoning Canal. No matter what John tried, however, he could not regain his early success. His responsibilities grew with the births of Oliver in 1839, and Peter in 1840. John began to search for a new kind of work. He traveled to the state of Virginia to speak with the managers of Oberlin College. Oberlin owned many acres of undeveloped land. John convinced the managers to let him survey and buy some of the land. The acreage that he wanted had running water in a spring that would support a tannery. In a foolish move, John used some of his partners' money in his private deals. In 1842 the partners sued John. That forced John to declare bankruptcy. The partners won their suit, but they did not receive much money. John had little to give.

In that same year, John moved the family to Richfield, Ohio. He had lost all of his land, and his farm was sold at auction. The Browns had only their beds, blankets, utensils, some food, and a few animals. The herd included 19 sheep that the court had ordered John to give to one of his partners. John would later work off that debt. He kept the sheep and hoped to build a large flock.

In 1843, John formed a partnership with a rich merchant named Simon Perkins. The two men put their sheep together in one herd. Perkins provided the Browns a house near his mansion. In return, the Browns cared for the sheep and sheared their wool. Then John sold the wool for the best price, and he and Perkins shared the money evenly. John wrote to his grown son, John Jr. excited about the agreement that would help "the poor bankrupt and his family."

John Brown could use the new developments in transportation to help move his wool to market. In the 1820s and 1830s, the United States continued to grow. Its transportation system grew right along with it. Railroads carried train cars filled with goods from the Midwest to the busy eastern states. Big boats made the trip on the Great Lakes. The Erie Canal opened in 1825 to carry boats back and forth from New York City to Buffalo and across Lake Erie to Ohio. By the time Perkins-Brown opened for business, both trains and boats could transport loads of wool.

The future held promise, and John continued to be a loving father to his many children. Then even greater losses occurred. All of the children became ill with dysentery in September of 1843. John helped nurse them, as Mary had just given birth and was ill herself. Charles, age six, was the first to die. Austin, the newborn, then three-year old Peter, and nine-year old Sarah, followed Charles. John wrote to John Jr., of his great sorrow. He told him, "Four of our number sleep in the dust, and were all buried together in one grave." He called his sadness a "bitter cup" from which the whole family "[drank] deeply." Helping to console them was the birth of a daughter, Annie.

John knew that life must go on. In 1844 he left the family to work in Akron, Ohio, to build a strong line of quality sheep. Wool merchants soon learned of the Perkins-Brown flock. John became so qualified as a wool producer that he wrote a manual instructing others. Devoted to his herd, he gave them special care. His daughter Ruth once wrote that when newborn lambs

John wished that he could do more to support the antislavery movement. There were others who believed just as strongly that an end to slavery would give slaves unfair advantages against white citizens.

suffered from the cold, her father brought them into the house. He would put a freezing lamb in warm water, rub it, and wrap it in a blanket.

In order to buy more sheep, John traveled throughout the Ohio Valley. During 1844 and 1845, the year John's daughter, Ameilia, was born, the farmers of Ohio and Virginia came to know him well. John discussed the problems they all experienced while caring for their animals. He developed a plan for all of the farmers to work together in a group called a cooperative, or co-op. They would share their expenses and their profits, the money made from wool sales. The farmers asked John to head the co-op.

John and John Jr. traveled to Springfield, Massachusetts. There John planned to set up a center to store and sell the wool. His other grown sons, Jason and Owen, would stay in Akron to care for the Perkins-Brown flock. Mary moved to Akron as well. She still had a family to raise. She and John now had three boys, Watson, Salmon, and Oliver. They also had three-year-old Annie, and little Amelia. When John left for Springfield in 1846, Mary was again pregnant. Baby Sarah, who was named after the daughter who died, was born two months after John departed.

At the Springfield center, the Browns worked hard on the business. As he worked, John felt frustrated. He preferred to help the antislavery movement. He wished that he could match the moves of others, such as New York resident Gerrit Smith. In August 1846, Smith gave 3,000 farms in eight counties to 3,000 black men. Many were escaped slaves. John dreamed of living among those men and farming. Still, he made himself focus on his quickly growing business. John's luck seemed to have returned.

Then, once again, death reminded John that luck could quickly change. Ruth, who was 17 at the time, had returned from school to help Mary with the children. In a terrible accident, she spilled scalding water on Amelia, and the baby soon died.

Changes within the country also disturbed John. In May 1846 a group of American soldiers fought with a group of Mexican soldiers. The United States declared war against Mexico, hoping to gain more land. Some members of **Congress,** the law-making body of the United States, did not want the war. They felt its main purpose was to bring more land into the South and expand slavery. By September 1847 the war ended. Many Southerners demanded that slaveholders settle the large amount of land gained. They argued that Southerners had died in battle and deserved that land.

To John, the government appeared to be falling into the hands of slaveholders. In 1847 he wrote a letter to Mary expressing his anger. In the letter, he said, "I feel considerable regret that I have lived so many years and have in reality done so little to increase the amount of human happiness." Soon after writing that letter, John brought his family to New York. John and Mary decided that he must at last act. In the fall of 1848, John invited a famous ex-slave named Frederick Douglass to visit him in Springfield. Although only in his twenties, Douglass was a powerful black leader of the antislavery movement. He was self-educated and had written a popular book called *Narrative of the Life of Frederick Douglass* in 1845.

Douglass wrote about his first meeting with John Brown and his family. He described their small house set in a neighborhood of working people. Plain inside, the house had no curtains or

Frederick Douglass was a former slave and powerful leader in the antislavery movement. Douglass and John Brown met in 1948, when John invited him to his home to discuss a plan to liberate the slaves.

carpets. The meal was a poor man's meal, made up of cabbage, potatoes, and beef soup. Douglass felt amazed at the invitation to eat with a white family. His amazement grew as Mary waited on him at the table as she would any honored guest. But his greatest amazement came when John began to explain his plan for liberating the slaves.

A depiction by African-American painter Jacob Lawrence of the meeting between Brown and Douglass.

4

The Bloodshed Begins

J ohn carefully explained his three-part plan for freeing the slaves to Frederick Douglass. He said that he did not plan for the slaves to revolt and kill their masters. He wanted to work slowly to bring freedom over time. He wanted to use the Appalachian Mountains, which ran through several Southern states, as natural forts.

In the first stage, a few armed men would seek out safe places to hide in the hills. They would visit **plantations** and secretly plan an escape with a few bold slaves. When 100 men gathered together, stage two would begin. The volunteers would ask large numbers of slaves to join up. The bravest would help form an army in the Appalachians. Those who wanted to leave could travel on the Underground Railroad. The hill groups would grow with supplies given to them by abolitionists. Stage three would expand the area from which the slaves escaped. Slavery, as a way of life, would weaken. Slave owners would not want to invest in slaves who would just run away.

Douglass told John he doubted the plan. Slave owners would not stand by during the first stage. As soon as their slaves disappeared, they would come into the hills. They would capture or kill the antislavery volunteers. They would cut off the supplies the volunteers needed. Brown agreed that might happen. He still believed that some groups would survive. He told Douglass, "I have no better use for my life, than to lay it down in the cause of the slave." He added that God commanded him to help end slavery. Douglass departed, telling John that he feared only violence could end slavery.

John and John Jr. continued their work. In 1848 wool prices fell. The men who trusted John to sell their wool asked him to sell before the prices dropped lower. John told them he would wait until the price was right. Meanwhile, he visited Gerrit Smith, the man who offered farms to the blacks. John asked Smith whether he might buy some land in a group of mountains to the north called the Adirondacks. John thought of using the Adirondacks in his plan to free the slaves. The two men became close friends.

In May 1848, John and Mary welcomed another baby girl named Ellen. During September, John took Mary and Ellen to visit Mary's brother. He traveled on to North Elba, the part of New York where Smith offered land to the slaves. The frontier area reminded him of his move to Ohio as a child. As he traveled back to Springfield, John picked up Mary and Ellen along the way. Little Ellen caught pneumonia and became very ill. John held her for hours at a time. Ruth later told of hearing John singing to Ellen as he sat up with her

When John moved to North Elba, New York, he hired an ex-slave named Thomas Jefferson to help with the move and the work. He also hired two other workers and a housekeeper. In addition, the Browns took in an escaped slave. Ten people lived in the small farmhouse. The main floor held one large room used for both cooking and eating. Two people could also sleep in that room. The others slept in two rooms above the main floor. According to his neighbors, John never turned visitors away from a meal and a place to rest, in spite of the crowded conditions.

at night. Ellen could not survive the illness, and the Browns buried another child. Soon John, Mary, and the remaining small children—Watson, Oliver, Salmon, Sarah, and Annie—left the sadness of Springfield behind.

The Browns moved onto a North Elba farm that John rented from Smith. In July 1849 he made a trip to England, hoping to sell his and the other farmers' wool. This turned out to be the worst year for John to make the trip. He lost $40,000. Perkins and Brown closed, and John faced many angry customers.

John also faced disturbing events in the United States. In 1850 people rushed to the

territory of California to find gold. California's population grew from 5,000 to 80,000 in two years. Californians decided they wanted their territory to become a state and they wanted the new state to bar slavery. Many arguments took place in the U.S. Congress. Southerners objected to California being a free state. Some Southerners began to discuss the idea of **secession**, or withdrawing their states from the United States. In 1850 the South passed was the **Fugitive Slave Law**. The new law made catching runaway slaves the government's job. Special judges would watch to see whether Northerners helped to catch the slaves. Those who protected runaways could be punished.

The Browns and other abolitionists found the new law upsetting. They could no longer help runaways without breaking the law. John quickly wrapped up his business dealings. He stayed in New York to attend the wedding of his oldest daughter, Ruth, to a farmer named Henry Thompson. Then in 1852 John decided to move

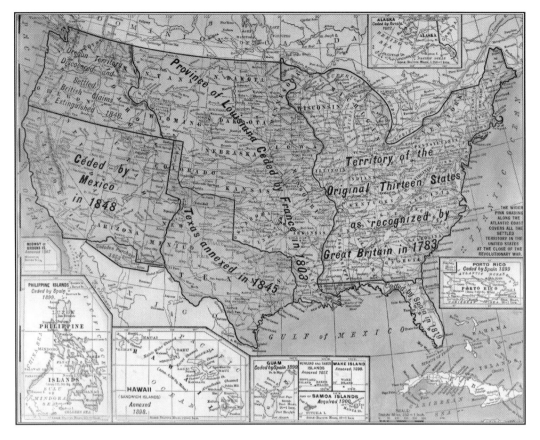

Many Americans believed in "Manifest Destiny." This was the concept that the United States was destined to reach from the Atlantic to the Pacific Ocean. This map shows how the United States looked in the 1800s. As the country grew, the question of whether or not new states would be free states, or allow slavery, became important.

his family back to the Western Reserve. Several unhappy customers of Perkins and Brown filed lawsuits. John traveled back and forth from Ohio to New York to attend the court hearings. He still worked in the antislavery movement. Also in 1852 an important book by Harriet Beecher Stowe, called *Uncle Tom's Cabin,* was published. Stowe's book showed the nation how horrible it was to be a slave. The book was fictional, but realistic. It attacked slavery by telling a story about slave families.

In his spare time in New York, John helped work against the Fugitive Slave Law. He wrote to Mary that in his time spent with the ex-slaves, he encouraged them to keep up hope. In 1851, John formed a new antislavery group. He called it the League of Gileadites. He took the name from the Bible story about Gideon, who picked 300 brave men to help him fight a group called the Midianites. John continued to take great pride in Mary and the children. They grieved together over the loss of another newborn boy. In 1854 they could celebrate the birth of John's last child, another girl named Ellen.

During John's travels in 1851, his younger sons cared for the Hudson farm. His sons, 16-year-old Watson, 15-year-old Salmon, and 12-year-old Oliver were hard workers. Annie, age eight, and five-year-old Sarah helped Mary in the house. The older boys, John Jr. and Jason, had farms and families of their own in Akron, Ohio. They also had to help Owen and Frederick run the Perkins farm. Owen had one crippled arm, and Frederick began to suffer from mental illness, as his mother had.

Over the years, many events had affected the antislavery movement. Arguments over whether new states in the growing country would be free states or slave states continued. One agreement, the Kansas-Nebraska Act, at last passed in 1854. The act divided the land called Nebraska territory into two states. Nebraska was formed from the northern part, and Kansas was formed from the southern part. State citizens could vote on whether to allow slavery. Both proslavery and antislavery people moved into Kansas. One antislavery group settled on the South Bank of the Kansas River. They named their settlement Lawrence. In 1855, John Jr., Jason, Owen, Frederick, and

Salmon Brown caught the "fever" to leave Ohio with their families. Their Aunt and Uncle Adair had already moved to the Kansas territory. The boys urged John and Mary to join them.

Almost immediately, violence erupted in Kansas. Missouri, the state to the south, was mostly a proslavery state. Groups from Missouri called Border Ruffians traveled north to frighten the antislavery Kansans. In 1855 a group of 5,000 Border Ruffians invaded Kansas, screaming curses and promising to kill abolitionists. By October 1855, Kansas called a meeting of free-state supporters. The men attending wrote a free-state constitution they planned to put in place in 1856.

Not all Southerners who moved to Kansas joined in the proslavery activities, even though they supported slavery. This proved true of the Doyle family from Tennessee. Pleasant Doyle and his wife Mahala settled with their six children on 100 Kansas acres in November 1855. They built a cabin on the northern side of the

Franklin Pierce was president of the
United States from 1853 to 1857, during
which time the question of slavery in the
Kansas-Missouri territory erupted into
violence.

Pottawatomie Creek. They did not yet know it, but the Brown brothers lived just to the north. During that same month, the Ruffians attacked the Lawrence settlement. The people in Lawrence fought the Ruffians and organized patrols to watch for more attacks.

The Border Ruffians continued to make trouble. They captured supplies coming to the new settlers. They stole animals from wagon trains and killed or wounded the travelers. One proslavery newspaper wrote about the attacks. It said, "We are determined to make Kansas a slave state; though our rivers should be covered with the blood of the victims . . . we will not be deterred from our purpose." John Jr. began to organize the antislavery settlers to be able to fight their attackers. When John Jr. wrote one of his older sons, asking his father to join him, John answered the call. He left Mary and the children in the care of Watson, one of his older sons, and departed to take weapons to his sons in Kansas.

The bitter winter of 1856 stopped the Ruffian attacks for a time. Then the Kansas convention met again. President Franklin Pierce called that meeting unlawful. The U.S. Congress ordered Kansas antislavery forces to halt their activities. John Brown Jr. served as a delegate to the convention and led a group of volunteer militia. He learned that a band of Ruffians intended to attack Lawrence again. Galloping across southern Kansas, he spread the word and met up with his father. As the group traveled to Lawrence, they passed through a town called Shermanville close to the Pottawatomie Creek. The Brown sons hated the people who lived there, including Pleasant Doyle and his family. Everyone knew of rumors that Shermanville residents often fed and housed the Ruffians.

After midnight on May 23, a messenger met the Browns. He explained that Ruffians had burned Lawrence to the ground without one shot fired. The fact that Lawrence surrendered without a fight made John Brown furious. He convinced some of the men it was time to fight back and punish the Ruffians and their supporters. John Jr. and his brothers had departed and did not know of their father's plan.

John and his travelers camped outside of Shermanville, plotting killing of their own. On the night of May 24, 1856, they entered the Doyles's cabin. According to 16-year-old John Doyle, John Brown took Pleasant Doyle and his two oldest sons outside of the cabin. When John Doyle went out late that night, he found the bodies of his father and brothers, stabbed and hacked to death with swords. Several of the Doyle neighbors also lay dead.

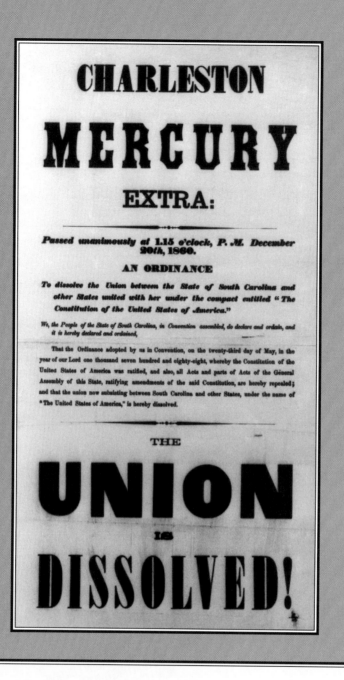

This broadside announces South Carolina's secession from the Union in 1861. More Southern states followed, forming the Confederate States of America. The Civil War between the North and South over slavery would soon begin.

Monster
or Hero?

ivil War threatened, as Kansas's antislavery forces grew stronger. John Brown and his volunteers became hunted criminals. They had become **guerillas**, men who attacked on their own and made their own laws. The Border Ruffians vowed to get these Pottawatomie Rifles, as John's men were called.

When John Jr. heard of the Pottawatomie murders, he broke down emotionally and resigned his leadership. Like their father, he and Jason believed in abolition, but not in murder. The Ruffians, knowing Jason was John's son, captured and almost hanged him. Luckily, a Kentucky judge saved his life. John Jr. also became a prisoner along with his brother at Osawatomie, Kansas. The boys endured a terrible march through the summer heat to Fort Leavenworth, Kansas. The guards soon released Jason, who rejoined his father. John Jr. remained in prison where he suffered beatings until September.

During this time, John Brown could do nothing to help his sons. He continued his raids and became an antislavery symbol to the Kansas **free-staters**. The Kansas Free-State assembly met again, despite the government's orders against their meetings. John made the decision instead to fight to the end. Sickened by the fighting and killing, all of John's sons except for Frederick decided to leave the territory. Jason would wait for John Jr.'s dismissal from prison. John and Frederick escorted Owen, Salmon, Oliver, and Henry to the Kansas border.

One morning, while unarmed, Frederick met some Ruffians as he cared for horses at his uncle's home. He commanded them to stop, but they fired a single bullet into his heart. The Frederick's 12-year-old son, Charles, rode through nearby Osawatomie and to John Brown's camp warning of the raiders. John and his militia fired on the raiders, but could not drive them away. They destroyed Osawatomie. By September 1856 people had had enough of the bloodshed. A new anitslavery political party called the Republicans formed, hoping to stop the violence.

A welcome lull in the fighting occurred by September, the month of John Jr.'s release from prison. John decided to return home where the family could grieve together for Frederick. Sick with fever, he rode in the back of a wagon as John Jr. and Jason cared for him. By March 1857 thousands of new free-staters crossed into Kansas. The proslavery forces had failed in their efforts to make Kansas a slave territory.

While at home in the east, John decided that perhaps he should gather militia in Missouri. As he told a friend, "It was only fair, as Missouri had [tried] to make a slave state of Kansas . . . that Kansas should make a free state of Missouri." John chose the town of Tabor in Iowa to begin gathering supplies. He stored his guns at a house owned by Reverend John Todd who introduced John to wealthy Boston men. These men, later known as the "Secret Six," raised money for the antislavery cause. John gained about $20,000 in money and supplies. He hired a military teacher to train his volunteers.

During 1857, John tried to save money for his family in case he was killed. Mary, Ellen, Sarah, and Annie still lived on the North Elba farm. John asked his supporters for $1,000, and he bought the farm from Gerrit Smith. He also wanted to be sure that people remembered him in an honorable way. He moved the gravestone of the grandfather killed in the Revolutionary War to North Elba. Before departing, he had Frederick's name inscribed on the stone. He requested that his own name be added, if he died as a soldier. John decided that his first battle in the South would

John chose Virginia as the first Southern state in which he would do battle to end slavery. This state would eventually be home to the capital of the Confederacy— Richmond, which is shown here at the time of the Civil War.

take place in Virginia, although his men had expected to return to Kansas.

John helped with the hauling of the supplies and weapons 200 miles across Iowa to

Springfield. He left his men training in December 1857 and traveled east to meet with Frederick Douglass. At that time Douglass lived in Rochester, New York, where John stayed to write a constitution. He hoped to put it to use once he gained strength in the Southern states. Even John's devoted followers argued that the odds against them were enormous. They feared the Southern states would bring their own troops and U. S. troops against Brown. In spite of their fears, John remained unmoved. He believed that he carried out God's wishes.

John opened a convention in Chatham, Canada, home for a large number of escaped slaves, in May 1858. He gained the support of the black community who approved most of his constitution without argument. John made clear that he hoped not to dissolve the United States, but to strengthen it by removing slavery. He did have one problem. The Secret Six wanted the weapons they paid for used in Kansas, as planned. John reluctantly returned to Lawrence, in June 1858.

For the most part, violence had disappeared from Kansas. Soon after John arrived, however, Border Ruffians killed a number of free-state settlers. One survivor, Elias Snyder, invited John to camp at his farm. John used the name Shubel Morgan, and his volunteers moved onto the farm in July. They waited several weeks to defend the area, but that Ruffian attack proved to be the final one. Again sick with a fever, John recovered at his sister's cabin at Osawatomie. He raised money for the cause through November. Hearing of a hunt for an escaped slave, John raided two Missouri plantations in December. Once again, John and his men became criminals.

In 1859, John made a crucial decision to begin his Southern invasion at Harpers Ferry, Virginia. A building there, the **armory**, held many weapons belonging to the U.S. government. He would capture the weapons to use against proslavery forces. His raid would let the Southern slaves know that friends had arrived. The plan shocked many of the volunteers, but in the end, they all decided to stick with John. Although still unhappy about the fighting, Oliver, Owen, and Watson remained loyal to their father. Owen and one group of men would travel apart from John's forces, joining them at the armory.

On October 16, 1859, John took his sons and 15 other volunteers into Harpers Ferry. When the fight broke out, rumors spread. One person reported that a group of 150 men had attacked the town. Government forces arrived quickly and surprised John. Soon, the local militia joined them. This large group prevented Owen from carrying out his plans. John waited all morning on October 17 for additional volunteers. Only a few men appeared, and by 2:00 P.M., John could not escape. One volunteer with a white flag emerged from the armory building that sheltered the volunteers, requesting a **truce**. He was taken prisoner and locked up. Next, John sent Watson out. Almost immediately, Watson was struck by an enemy bullet. He crawled back to the armory. In the shooting that followed, men on both sides died. Oliver Brown lay beside his brother Watson. By the time night fell, only four men remained alive with John.

On the morning of October 18, troops knocked down the armory door. Three minutes later, John lay bleeding from sword cuts, and the remaining volunteers were dead or captured. When asked why he had done it, John replied, "We came to free the slaves, and only that."

The officials knew that John would be a dangerous prisoner. He would continue to speak against slavery, every word appearing in newspapers. Around the country, people discussed John and Harpers Ferry. The officials hurriedly planned John's trial for October 25. John had

During John's trial, his lawyer received a message. It explained that mental illness existed in the Brown family. The lawyer mentioned this in court, because people who committed crimes due to mental illness could avoid execution. John stood up to protest. He feared that if people thought him crazy, the antislavery movement could be harmed. The court dismissed the argument, and John missed that chance to save his life.

President Lincoln is shown reading the Emancipation Proclamation during the Civil War to members of his Cabinet in September 1862. The final proclamation was issued on January 1, 1863, and freed slaves in the Confederate states that were in rebellion.

little time to develop a defense. He could not even recover from his wounds by the time the trial began. His only hope lay in the fact that many people now felt sympathy for him. On October 26, John and his men were charged with murder and plotting a slave rebellion.

On October 31, the jury found John guilty. When asked if he wanted to speak, John explained that he only wanted to free the slaves. He never meant to murder anyone or destroy property. He agreed that he had turned to violence for his cause. He argued, however, that had he done it for the rich and powerful, he would not have to be convicted. The court ruled that John would hang on Friday December 2, 1859.

John spent his remaining days visiting with crowds who gathered at his cell. He wrote many letters to friends and family. He assured John Jr. that he did not fear death. John wrote in his last letter to Mary that he would sacrifice more than his life if he could. On December 1, Mary visited him in jail, and they shared a final supper. Just before his hanging, John handed a note to a guard. He stated that he felt sure that there would have been bloodshed before "the crimes of this guilty land" would ever end.

John Brown did not abolish slavery as he set out to. Not until Lincoln freed the slaves with the

"The Tragic Prelude," a mural by John Steuart Curry, hangs in the Topeka, Kansas State Capitol. It depicts John Brown's life-long fight against slavery.

Emancipation Proclamation on January 1, 1863, would that occur. Some people called John a monster, while others viewed him as a hero. Whatever people thought of John Brown, he played a crucial role in the movement known as abolition.

GLOSSARY

abolitionist-a person wanting to abolish, or end, slavery.

armory-a building that stores weapons.

congress-any gathering of individuals for the purpose of creating rules of government.

depression-a period when a nation produces few goods, many workers are unemployed, and many businesses fail.

execution-the ending of a person's life as punishment for crimes committed.

free-staters-people who wanted newly created states to outlaw slavery.

fugitive-a person in hiding after breaking a law.

Fugitive Slave Laws-laws that allowed slave owners to reclaim runaway slaves.

guerilla-a person who fights for a cause apart from an organized military group.

plantation-huge southern farm using slave labor to produce mainly cotton during the 1800s.

rebellion-a fight for freedom.

secession-to withdraw from a group.

territory-land belonging to the United States that is not part of an existing state.

truce-an agreed upon peace.

Underground Railroad-a system of people and places that helped slaves escape to freedom.

CHRONOLOGY

1800	John Brown born in Connecticut on May 29.
1805	Family moves to Hudson, Ohio.
1818–25	Works as a tanner in Hudson, Ohio.
1821	Marries Dianthe Lusk on June 21; John Brown Jr., born.
1822–24	Births of Jason, and Owen.
1825–35	Works as tanner and postmaster in Randolph, Pennsylvania.
1827–30	Births of Frederick, Ruth, and unnamed son.
1831	Frederick dies. Unnamed son given name Frederick.
1832	Newborn dies. Dianthe dies.
1833	Marries Mary Anne Day, July 11.
1834–36	Moves to Franklin, Ohio. Births of Watson, Salmon, and Sarah.
1836–37	Loss of money and property. Moves to Hudson, Ohio. Birth of Charles (1837).
1839–41	Works as a sheep farmer. Births of Oliver and Peter.
1842–43	Declares bankruptcy. Moves to Richfield, Ohio. Birth of Austin. Forms Perkins Brown. Deaths of Charles, Peter, Austin, and Sarah.
1844–46	Birth and death of Amelia. Birth of Annie. Birth of second daughter named Sarah.

1847–48	Discusses slave revolt with Frederick Douglass. Birth and death of Ellen.
1854	Birth of second daughter named Ellen. Five sons move to Kansas in October.
1856	Sacking of Lawrence and Pottawatomie murders. John Jr. and Jason in Kansas prison, then released.
1857	Raises money in New England.
1859	Visits Canada. Harpers Ferry attack, October. Frederick and Owen killed. Trial, October 27–November 4. Imprisoned forty days. Executed December 2. Buried December 8.

CIVIL WAR TIME LINE

1860   Abraham Lincoln is elected president of the United States on November 6. During the next few months, Southern states begin to break away from the Union.

1861   On April 12, the Confederates attack Fort Sumter, South Carolina, and the Civil War begins. Union forces are defeated in Virginia at the First Battle of Bull Run (First Manassas) on July 21 and withdraw to Washington, D.C.

1862   Robert E. Lee is placed in command of the main Confederate army in Virginia in June. Lee defeats the Army of the Potomac at the Second Battle of Bull Run (Second Manassas) in Virginia on August 29–30. On September 17, Union general George B. McClellan turns back Lee's first invasion of the North at Antietam Creek near Sharpsburg, Maryland. It is the bloodiest day of the war.

1863   On January 1, President Lincoln issues the Emancipation Proclamation, freeing slaves in Southern states. Between May 1–6, Lee wins an important victory at Chancellorsville, but key Southern commander Thomas J. "Stonewall" Jackson dies from wounds. In June, Union forces hold the city of Vicksburg, Mississippi, under siege. The people of Vicksburg surrender on July 4. Lee's second invasion of the North during July 1–3 is decisively turned back at Gettysburg, Pennsylvania.

1864   General Grant is made supreme Union commander on March 9. Following a series of costly battles, on June 19 Grant successfully encircles Lee's troops in Petersburg, Virginia. A siege of the town lasts nearly a year.

Union general William Sherman captures Atlanta on September 2 and begins the "March to the Sea," a campaign of destruction across Georgia and South Carolina. On November 8, Abraham Lincoln wins reelection as president.

1865   On April 2, Petersburg, Virginia, falls to the Union. Lee attempts to reach Confederate forces in North Carolina but is gradually surrounded by Union troops. Lee surrenders to Grant on April 9 at Appomattox, Virginia, ending the war. Abraham Lincoln is assassinated by John Wilkes Booth on April 14.

FURTHER READING

Bial, Raymond. *The Underground Railroad.* Boston: Houghton Mifflin, 1999.

Cox, Clinton. *Fiery Vision: The Life and Death of John Brown.* New York: Scholastic Trade, 1997.

Redpath, James. *Public Life of Captain John Brown, with autobiography of his childhood and youth.* Manchester, New Hampshire: Ayer Co., 2001.

Scott, John Anthony, and Robert Alan Scott. *John Brown of Harpers Ferry.* New York: Facts on File, 1988.

Stanley, Jerry. *Hurry Freedom: African Americans in Gold Rush California.* New York: Crown Publishers, 2000.

PICTURE CREDITS

INDEX

ABOUT THE AUTHOR

VIRGINIA BRACKETT earned her Ph.D. in English from the University of Kansas and teaches college writing and literature. In addition to over 100 articles and stories for both academic and popular readerships, juveniles and adults, she has published several books, including *Jeff Bezos* (Chelsea House); *Classic Love and Romance Literature* (ABC-Clio); *Elizabeth Cary: Writer of Conscience* (Morgan Reynolds), included in the New York Public Library's 1997 catalog of recommended reading for teens; and *The Contingent Self* (Purdue University Press). She's at work on a biography of F. Scott Fitzgerald for Morgan Reynolds and a manuscript entitled *Early Women Writers: Voices from the Margins.*